I0191475

Disquiet

K. S. Shaw

/ BookLeaf
Publishing

India | USA | UK

Made with ♥ on the BookLeaf Publishing Platform
www.bookleafpub.in
www.bookleafpub.com

Dedication

For the ones who cry alone and still RISE.

Preface

In the quiet between heartbreak and healing, there is a voice. It is raw, unfiltered, and unafraid. *Disquiet* is a collection of poems that dwell in the spaces we often avoid where longing, betrayal, solitude, and the fragile hope intersect. These verses are not meant to soothe but to stir. They are the calls of a soul that has loved deeply, lost fiercely, and still chooses to speak.

This book is for the ones who cry alone, who build bridges with bare hands, who search for truth in eyes rather than words. It is for those who have been told they are too much, too broken, too loud and kept going anyway.

Let these poems be your mirror, your balm, a not so quiet rebellion.

Acknowledgements

To the women who taught me how to survive silence. To the ones who taught me what not to settle for and held space for my unraveling. To the readers who find themselves in these lines.

You are not alone.

1. Disquiet

When
I see you
There is a pause
Accompanied by pain
that lingers
Long after you leave
Your presence
evades my space
Days after you leave
Emulating there could
Be a forever.
Yet shadows whisper
of fleeting moments,
Echoes of laughter
that dance in the air,
Like ghosts of a wish
too fragile to hold,
Each heartbeat a reminder
of what could have been.

2. In the Midst

A storm within my heart,
Your whispers linger,
Ravaging me.
In silence I seek solace,
In near memories,
Your gentle caress,
Morph into pain.
I chase shadows,
That you refuse to follow.
From the height of passion
I plummeted into a self-made abyss,
I yearn you,
All of you,
Yet you only need
From me
A temporary fix.
In the corners of dusk,
Where light meets despair,
I anchor my dreams,
But they drift like leaves,
Caught in a tempest,
As memories fade,
I listen still
For remnants of you.

A wisp of hope
Silence answers back,
A heart
Left wanting,
Unraveled,
Cut raw.

3. Standards

This ain't no love connection
When we are apart there is no love lost
You possess my mind
but never understand me
A broken paper doll
In a glue less world
Yearning for sea legs
To sail on down the road
Like the Commodores
Crying and begging like the Isleys
Brother this isn't no Ohio playing
Bald headed games in disguise
Of love
Hiding the pain and failure
Of no being wife material.

Still searching for solace
In echoes of laughter,
While shadows of doubt
Dance through my heart.
Each promise a whisper,
Each touch a scar,
Navigating silence,
Like a ship lost at sea.

In the twilight of dreams,
I gather the pieces,
Crafting a soul
That's fierce and free.
You may hold my mind,
But never my spirit—
A tempest of will,
No anchor to your shore.

4. Yet

Is 'Happily Ever After'
A bewitched thought
With a Cinderella Twist
Built to destroy
Or control
Little girls
'Til they grow up
Never to know better
What's the stitch?
Love still ain't saved me yet.

A fairy tale spun
In a web of regret,
They dance to the music,
But the strings,
They forget.
With dreams painted in gold,
Nearby shadows lurk,
They chase after whispers,
Yet the truth is unclear.

Behind every smile,
A tear left unshed,
In the kingdom of visions,

Where hopes often bled.
Beneath starry skies,
Where wishes are cast,
Are the futures,
That silence the past.

5. Cry

When I cry,
I cry alone,
Not for the pity of it.
But because the echo of my tears
Is the only thing that stays.

Everyone that I gave love to is gone,
Took pieces of me as souvenirs,
Left silence where their laughter lived.

I build bridges with my bare hands,
Only to watch them burn
Under the weight of footsteps
I thought always would return.

Crying ain't weakness,
It's the rain washing my roots
The tide that softens the edges
Of the jagged memories I carry.

So when I cry,
I cry alone,
For the beauty of holding
What's left of me

And calling it enough.

Yet in the stillness,
I find a spark,
A flicker of hope,
In the fragments of love
That whisper through the dark.

Each tear a testament,
Each sigh a song,
Woven into the fabric
Of where I've learned to belong.

So I let them fall,
Every glimmer and glisten,
A mosaic of sorrow,
An invitation to listen.

6. Stagnant

I need you

I need you, the reason

not because the world is lonely
but because you make it full
your hands turn silence into sound
and stillness into warmth

there is a space
that only you can fill
a soft place inside me
where your love settles
without asking for permission

you are the quiet answer
to questions I never knew I had
the light that comes through
when I forget
how to see myself

I do not need the world
when I have you
because you are the reason

I understand
what love is

7. I Want You

I don't want love,
I want truth in your eyes,
Not the promises made,
But the fire that survives.
No roses or moonlight,
No sweet serenades,
Just the depth of your soul,
No parades or charades.
I don't want the words,
I want what they mean,
The quiet,
Between the real,
Can be seen.
Not the fantasy painted,
But the raw and the real,
The scars and the laughs,
The wounds that still heal.

8. Untitled

My soul screams
HELP
No ears to hear
An abyss of sadness
extending from the brink
of joyless existence

Unfair circumstances
Leaving me
Abandoned
Broken
Losing
No one hears
I lie to myself
Truthfully
No one cares.

I search
for a hand,
a heartbeat,
a glimmering thread,
to weave through the dark,
to shatter this cage,
and let me breathe again.

9. Inheritance

I carry my mother's silence
Like a locket around my throat,
Her sighs tucked in my pockets,
Her warnings stitched into my coat.
She taught me to smile
With clenched teeth,
To love
Without asking for return.
Now I pass down
The ache she gave me,
Wrapped in velvet,
Soft and sharp.
I whisper her tales
When the night falls,
Her strength softly calls.
Each word,
a fiber
In the fabric of scars,
Binding the past
With the light of who we are.

10. Weight

Want is a heavy thing
It drags behind me
Like a suitcase
Stuffed with maybe.
I unpack it
In empty rooms,
Lay it out

Each crumpled hope,
A whispered prayer,
Fills the silence,
A weight I wear.
Shadows gather,
Flickering thoughts,
In every corner,
A battle fought.

I clip my dreams
To the wall with pins,
Watch them flutter,
Straining for wins.
I pause,
As time unfolds,
My story untold.

11. No Vacancy

I made space for you
In every corner of me,
Evicted my peace
To house your chaos.
Now I hang a sign: No Vacancy.
Not for others,
Not for games,
Not for a love
That forgets my name.

12. The Quiet Kind

I don't scream anymore.
I whisper.
I write.
I bleed in metaphors
And stitch myself
With syllables.
This is the quiet kind of survival
The kind that doesn't beg
To be seen
But dares you
To look anyway
I crumble into verses,
Each line a pulse,
A heartbeat caught
In the space between breaths.
Crafting light from darkness,
Imprints of a soul
That knows the weight of silence.
Listen close,
For in the stillness lies
The roar of a thousand unsaid truths,

13. Rewritten

I rewrote my story
Without you in it.
Changed the ending,
Burned the prologue,
Kept the lessons.
Now I walk
Without waiting,
Love
Without losing,
Living
Without apology.
In the silence,
I found my voice,
A symphony of choices,
Hope.
Each step forward
A dance of freedom,
Embracing emptiness,
Chasing the dawn.
I write my own chapter,
Where I am enough,
A tale rewritten,
With resilience ink.

14. The Lie of Closure

They said closure would come
Like a sunrise.
But it came
Like a slammed door.
No light.
No warmth.
Just everything
I didn't get to say.

Again, who is they?

15. Unsent

I wrote you letters
I never mailed.
Each one
A confession,
A wound,
A wish.
They sit in a drawer
Like unwanted change
Of a love
That never learned
To stay.

16. Shaping Alone

Alone isn't empty.
It's shaped like me
Curled on the couch,
Laughing at my own jokes,
Dancing in the kitchen
With no one watching.
Not a void.
Victory.
Symphony of silence,
Where secrets become songs,
Moments stretch like shadows,
There is joy in the stillness,
Dreams fall from the air,
Embracing the warmth of solitude.
A tapestry of thoughts,
Fragile
Rare
I sip reflection,
a sweet drink,
In the depths of my mind,
I create space,
To think.
Each heartbeat
a rhythm,

Each sigh
a refrain,
Safety crafted into restructured pain,
Between the walls,
My spirit can soar,
Alone not lonely
Richer than before.

17. Quiet Shift

I used to chase
The loudest joy.
Newly minted
I seek peace.
Sliding into place
That can't shout.
Tranquility,
It settles.
And I settle with it.
Stillness wavers,
Through the quiet air.
A gentle balm,
Unrushed,
Unbent,
Where noise once lingered.
I inhale
Sweet grace.

18. What I know NOW

I know now
That love
Is not
LOUD
It is
consistent
kind
It does not
VANISH
When the lights go out
I know now
That I am
I AM
ENOUGH
Even when
NO ONE
says so

19. Strength

I thought strength
Was holding it all together.
It is strength
Letting it fall
Without shame.
It is strength
After the break
The choice
To begin again.
It is strength
Finding beauty
In the shattered pieces,
Learning to dance
On the fragments,
With a heart
That dares to hope,
Writing new stories
It is strength
Pulling me
From the ashes
Of what once was.
To a phoenix
Of what is to come.

20. Last Page

I don't have
All the answers.
But I have
This moment.
And that
Is enough
To begin.

.